SRA Open Court Reading

First Reader

Grade K

McGraw Hill Education

Program Authors

Carl Bereiter, Ph.D.

Andrew Biemiller, Ph.D.

Joe Campione, Ph.D.

Doug Fuchs, Ph.D.

Lynn Fuchs, Ph.D.

Steve Graham, Ph.D.

Karen Harris, Ph.D.

Jan Hirshberg, Ed.D.

Anne McKeough, Ph.D.

Marsha Roit, Ed.D.

Marlene Scardamalia, Ph.D.

Marcy Stein, Ph.D.

Gerald H. Treadway Jr, Ph.D.

Photo Credits

64 Image Source; **65** JGI/Jamie Grill/Getty Images, McGraw-Hill Education; **66** Brandy Taylor/Getty Images, Eclipse Studios/McGraw-Hill Education; **67** McGraw-Hill Education, ©Corbis.

MHEonline.com

Send all inquiries to:
McGraw-Hill Education
8787 Orion Place
Columbus, OH 43240

ISBN: 978-0-07-669108-1
MHID: 0-07-669108-X

Printed in the United States of America.

1 2 3 4 5 6 7 8 9 ROV 21 20 19 18 17 16 15

First Reader

Table of Contents

Vote for President!

by Dennis Fertig
illustrated by Scott R. Brooks

In the United States, we choose our president. We vote every four years. How does it work?

People ask and ask. Who is best for president? One candidate tells her plans for the United States. A group likes her plans. She is best for president!

The other candidate tells his plans for the United States. A different group likes his plans. He is best for president! Who will be the next president?

In towns, she tells her plans. She asks for votes. In towns, he tells his plans. He asks for votes. They both talk to lots of people.

On TV, he talks and she talks. People sit and ask, "Is she best for president? Is he?"

LIVE DEBATE

It is time for all the people to vote. They will choose who is best for the United States. They will vote for the next president!

Teddy's Bears

by Thomas Birch
illustrated by Peter Francis

Most kids have cute teddy bears. Kids like them. But who gave teddy bears that name? Why teddy?

Long ago, Theodore Roosevelt was president of the United States. He liked to hunt. He hunted with his pals.

On a trip, his pals trapped an old bear. The president felt bad for the bear. He did his best to save the bear's life.

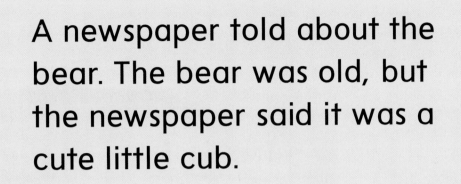

A newspaper told about the bear. The bear was old, but the newspaper said it was a cute little cub.

A man saw the newspaper. He sold stuffed bears in his shop. He called them "Teddy's bears." Teddy was the president's nickname.

Kids liked Teddy's bears. The man sold a lot of them. But people called them "teddy bears." We still do!

A Feathered Friend

by Phillip Frederick
illustrated by Soud

President Thomas Jefferson had a pet mockingbird. His name was Dick. Dick spent a lot of time with Thomas. But he hid if the president had a visitor.

Yet when Thomas was free,
he would call down his pet.

Thomas might grab a fiddle and play for a bit. His pet sat on the desk and sang a good song. Not all mockingbirds can sing well. Dick did.

A president must work. So at times, Thomas had to tell his pet mockingbird that. Then Dick just sat with Thomas.

Dick still sang to Thomas. Then Thomas might hum a bit.

If a man came in, the bird sat and hid. Could the man tell that a mockingbird sat up there? He might not. But Thomas could.

President Me?

by Nicole Hatfield
illustrated by Nomar Perez

President Ross is on TV.

He is as smart as smart can be.

I like his speech. I like his voice.

If I could vote, he'd be my choice.

LIVE

22

I can be the president too.
Some big hopes really can come true!
Will President Ross vote for me?
I will just have to wait and see.

Red, Yellow, Blue

by Joseph Phelan
illustrated by Eric Comstock

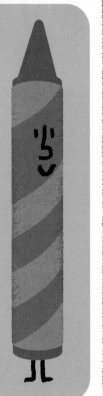

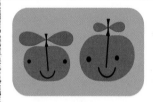

Do you like this color?

Can you name it?

Yes, it is red!

24

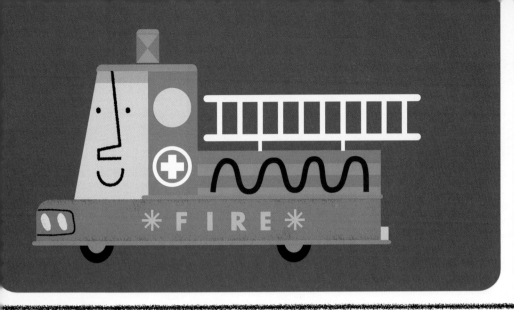

We see red a lot.

What red snacks do you like?

What kind of truck is red?

What can a red sign tell you?

MARKET

APPLES

Do you like this color?

Can you name it?

Yes, it is yellow!

Look at all the yellow!

What yellow stuff do we eat?

What kind of bus is yellow?

Do you like this color?

Can you name it?

Yes, it is blue!

US MAIL

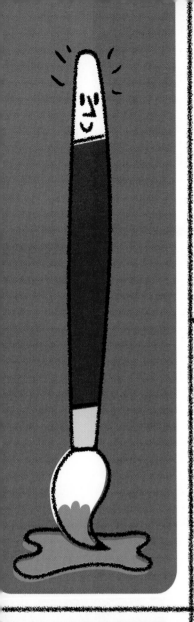

We see blue all the time.

When we look up, we see blue.

What is in that blue box?

Who is the woman in blue?

What do you like best, red, yellow, or blue?

29

Purple, Orange, Green, and Dan

by Jack Williams
illustrated by Gabriele Tafuni

Dan had cans of yellow.

Jan had cans of blue.

Bess had cans of red.

30

"We must make purple," said Bess.

"Mix blue and red," said Jan.

"That makes purple," said Dan.

"We must make orange," said Bess.

"Mix red and yellow," said Jan.

"That makes orange," said Dan.

"We must make green," said Bess.
"Mix blue and yellow," said Jan.
"That makes green," said Dan.

"If we mix purple with orange," said Bess.

"And add green," said Jan.

"What do we get?" said Bess.

"You get me!" said Dan.

"Yes!" said Bess.

"Yes!" said Jan.

Hide and Seek

by Dave Allyn
illustrated by Stephen Costanza

Hide-and-seek is fun!

Sal counts. The kids hide.

Sal looks for her pals.

"I see you, Ted," she yells.

Ted is sad.

"You always spot me," he tells Sal.

"I will tell you why," she tells him.

"Grass is green," Sal tells Ted.
"Plants are green.
Hills are brown and tan.
Rocks are gray."

Sal tells Ted, "Look at Sam.
He has on brown pants
and a tan top.
He blends into the hill."

39

Sal tells Ted, "Look at the other kids.
They have colors that blend.
Brown, tan, gray, and green blend in.
They help you hide."

Ted looks at his red pants and top.
"I must run home," he tells Sal.
"I must find hide-and-seek stuff!
Then I can blend in."

Essential Question What colors are opposites?

Black and White

by Charlie Barrett
illustrated by Steve Mack

A man in black rides his white bike.
I see him every day.

A man in white rides his black bike.
He rides the other way.

Can it be the same funny man?
Who likes both white and black?

Can the man have a funny plan
As he rides there and back?

Tom's Plans

by Carl Stein
illustrated by Mattia Cerato

"Look, I can make a plan,"

said Tom.

"I can make circles.

I can add a triangle.

We can make it!"

44

"That is a bike!" Nell said.
"There are lots of bikes and
bike plans."
That made Tom sad.
He made his next plan.

"Look, I made this plan," Tom said.
"It has circles. We can make it!"
"That is a van," said Nell.
"There are lots of vans."

Tom's next plan had a triangle.

It was on a box.

"That is a plan for a home," said Nell.

"We have homes!"

Then Tom hid his pad.

Nell did not see it.

She did see Tom's hands go fast.

She did see red, green, blue,
and yellow spots.

"This is not a plan!" said Tom.

"It is just fun to look at."

It made Nell smile.

"I like it Tom!" she said.

Plants in a Pattern

by Mark Tapia
illustrated by Courtney Autumn Martin

I help Mom plant our flowers.

She has yellow, purple, and red.

She will plant them next to the grass.

Mom asks for a red flower.

I hand it to her and she plants it.

She asks for a yellow flower.

She plants it.

Mom asks for a purple flower.

She plants it.

Then she asks for a red flower again.

Then she asks for yellow.

When she asks again for purple,

I get it!

Mom will plant the flowers like that.

She will make a red, yellow, and

purple line.

As Mom plants the purple,
I set plants by the grass.
I set them in a line.

I set all the plants in a line.

Mom sees it and smiles.

"A red, yellow, and purple line!

Thanks, Meg," she tells me.

Shapes and Patterns

by Orsolya Dalton
illustrated by Carolina Farías

A circle is a shape.

A triangle is a shape.

Shapes can be in a class.

What shapes can you see?

Shapes make a pattern.

Find the patterns on a rug.

On the rug, what shape is red?

What shape is blue?

What patterns can rug

shapes make?

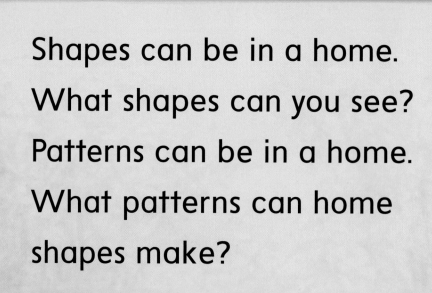

Shapes can be in a home.
What shapes can you see?
Patterns can be in a home.
What patterns can home
shapes make?

Shapes can be at camp.

What shapes do camp tents make?

Patterns can be at camp.

What patterns can you see?

Shapes can be on a street.

What shapes can you see?

Patterns can be on a street.

What patterns can you see?

THEATER

Shapes can be at a lake.

What shapes can you see?

Patterns can be at a lake.

What bright patterns can you see?

Essential Question How can shapes be helpful?

To the Game

by Steffan Munier
illustrated by Steve Mack

Are we late? Tick, tock!
What shape is this clock?

Green, red, black, and tan.
What shape is our van?

We cannot be late!
What shape is that gate?

Tickets at this stop!
What shape is on top?

Here at last!
Tick, tock!
What shape
is that clock?

Glossary

B

bit
a short while

bright
giving off light or having a strong color

C

choice
a decision made from two or more options

choose
to pick

circle
a closed, curved line

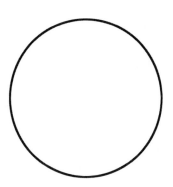

F

funny
strange or odd

G

good
positive; pleasing; healthy

H

hide
to keep out of sight

M

make
to cause to be

most
the biggest number of

P

pattern
the way in which colors, shapes, or lines repeat

plan
a drawing that shows how the parts of something go together

S

seek
to try to find

set
to place; put

song
the musical call of a bird

spot
to see

still
up to now

stuff
things of any sort

T

tickets
plural form of **ticket**: something that gives its owner the right to enter a place

triangle
a shape with three straight sides

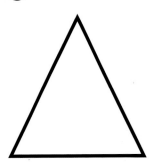

W

work
to make happen; to bring about